Hear The Cries Of My Heart

Taysean Wilson-Nolan

Published by FastPencil Publishing

Hear The Cries Of My Heart

First Edition

Print edition ISBN: 9781499906189

http://www.fastpencil.com

Printed in the United States of America

Table of Contents

HEAR
THE CRIES OF MY
HEART

Introduction

I was inspired to write "Hear the Cries of My Heart" during a wilderness season in my life. This was a period when I felt furthest away from God – His tangible presence, any plan He had for my life. At times I truly felt like there was no direction for me to turn; I was committed to continuing my walk in Christ, so resorting to any carnal thing wasn't an option for me. Furthermore, since it "felt" like God was absent in my life and His promises were even further, there was only one thing I could stand on in order to preserve myself, and that was the Word of God. I began to allow myself to be soaked in the gospel and at times I would feel the presence of God come over me, but only for a short while before leaving again.

After a few months, I began to feel a desire in my heart to begin writing a book concerning the deepest desires of my heart. I had the conviction that regardless of how difficult this season was, the Lord would eventually promote me, and the pain would cease. I wasn't sure yet if it was God who planted this desire in my heart. I had the understanding that when God is ready He'll empower me to do His will. I needed confirmation so I began to pray about it. The Lord told me, in my spirit, that it was Him who placed this desire in my heart. Once I heard this I was filled with excitement and I immediately began to write.

Many nights when I felt uneasy because of the circumstances I was in, I would remind myself of the true character of God by writing down every word that flowed out of my heart. In writing this book there was never a time when I had to analyze how I felt or reflect on my thoughts. I could hear the Spirit of the Lord speaking to me, bringing me peace, and transforming my mind as I wrote down every word.

Personally I feel like I share the experience of a reader every time I recite these poems and prayers. I often thought about King David, who found himself in the "temple" of God when he wrote hymns to the Lord. I found myself having a similar experience as I began to write this book and I relived every moment when I read it.

In writing "Hear the Cries of My Heart" I wanted to inspire others to seek Jesus with a fervent spirit when they're faced with difficulties. In the book of Acts, the Apostle Paul urges us "that we must through much tribulation enter into the kingdom of God" (Acts 14:22, King James Version). Every mighty man and woman of God was made by persevering through every harsh situation they were faced with. Our challenges in life are vital for our spiritual growth.

Part 1

Cries From The Wilderness

SECTION 1

I Surrender

The heart cries out from the wilderness. It says...

God, have you forsaken me? I don't know You here.

Just at that moment – suffering from the aridity of the dry land – my heart was brought in remembrance, so in repentance cried out: "God, You are my deliverer! O Lord, You took me from my shame and brought me into this arid place. You made me see my flaws and embrace Your perfection. Your presence secures me in this time of suffering. Redeem me, and remove my imperfections from Your sights – I am now Yours. Flow Your waters of life through me, so that I may never thirst in my spirit. You've brought me into this place, I can no longer only shame myself. Hear my cry in the wilderness, O Lord; if I have You I am convinced I have everything I need."

The seasons in our lives when we tend to feel the most unfulfilled, internally dry, and void – being absent from the presence of God and feeling further away from His promises - are the times when His work is most at hand. Throughout the Bible, we see the relationship between a person's suffering, the refining of their character, and their glory (achievements). Job gained the wisdom to become content in his suffering and trust in God's wisdom. Job says:

"Behold, I go forward, but he is not there, and backward, but I do not perceive him; on the left hand when he is working, I do not behold him; he turns to the right hand, but I do not see him. But he knows the way that I take; when he has tried me, I shall come out as gold" (Job 23:8-10, English Standard Version). My own experience has taught me that patience in Christ comes by endurance through our trials and labors. While I began to seek God in hopes of accomplishing my goals, He shifted my focus from the prize and toward Him. When my eyes were turned on Jesus, my heart turned away from my dreams, and the source of my life became God.

A Call of Desperation

The heart began to scream out in desperation...

O Lord, I have seen that even the harvest won't last; so where I am going cannot save me. There is no work I can do that will make me right before You.

"Surely every man walks about like a shadow; surely they busy themselves in vain; he heaps up riches, and does not know who will gather them. 'And now, Lord, what do I wait for? My hope is in You' " (Psalms 39:6, 7, New King James Version).

My God, let me know You intimately. In my emptiness, I long for Your every last word. When I am thirsty, I will seek Your guidance; I know You will lead me to the waters of life. Even in my shame, I do not search the world, but I turn to You and I am covered. Good Father, You are the redeemer of my soul. So, I cry to You in this wilderness; my desire is to see Your face.

Author Reflection

At 19 years old, I had an interaction with Jesus Christ that changed my life forever. The Lord led me into a new season where He took me out of my comfort zone. I was brought into a very dry place in my life. Every day was a struggle and whenever things appeared to get better it was only matter of time before they got even worse.

When I began to write I found contentment. The prayers I wrote down were the songs of my heart. The Spirit witnessed to me every promise of the Lord and every word I wrote settled a place in my heart.

Shadow of My Past

The heart begins to shout in joy. It says...

Lord, You desire not my own works, intelligence, authority, self-preservation, independence, or strength. You desire for me to surrender to You so that I may inherit everything You've promised me. While I slept, You made my dreams real and moved in my helplessness – my soul was brought to satisfaction. You became my refuge, not at the moment I suffered, but at the instant when I surrendered. Lord, You have brought me comfort in my desolation and filled me up so that I had no more voids.

The shadows of my past have followed me all my life; they established strongholds and convinced me that by the power of my own hands I could be saved. In chasing my own desires I followed the wind. I sustained myself in my own strength, but the burden on my heart was too much too carry. I began to stumble in my own way as my hands became weak and my mind became restless. My sight began to fail me and I could no longer see my way. But Father, You have seen my burdens. They've blinded me to Your promise! They love all things that are old and hate anything new. But I haven't forgotten the Word of my God. So I lay down all my burdens on Him. I am sustained by the hand of the Lord; He shall never permit me to move. My God became the light that overcame every shadow! So I know that Your reward wasn't any carnal thing but the fullness of Your presence.

A CALL FOR LEADERSHIP

The heart cries out to the Lord in passion...

Abba, Father, let Your kingdom pour out of me – I open myself to You – that I may be filled with Your Spirit. Let me see what You see, so that I may walk Your walk. The person You've called is held by the righteousness of Your hand, so that he may be exalted and prosperous in every way. He does not decide where he takes his next step, he allows the Lord to direct his ways. Nor does he love his life, but he loses for Christ's sake – gaining life everlasting. He does not seek wisdom from man but discerns all things as the Spirit of God witnesses to his own spirit; all secrets are made known to him. He is drawn by worldly possessions but suffers in his flesh so that he may be fruitful for thc kingdom of God. He seeks the Lord all his days and resides in the covenant of God.

Fruit of Meekness

The heart cries out fretfully...

Lord, I am filled with much passion. But don't let my impatience become my downfall. Bring tranquility and meekness back into me. Do not let me be enticed by temporal things. Your plan was to draw me closer to You – don't allow me to become distracted along the way. You honor those who've heard Your Word and keep Your commands. Not one will lack!

THE STRONG TOWER

The heart screams out in authority because it has found the heart of God. All those who receive Him in their heart will never be lost. The name of the Lord is a place of refuge for all of His who are troubled.

The heart begins to cry out in power...

O Lord, in You I have found my way; in You I have found the power. You gave me life; my soul is fulfilled and my joy is everlasting. My strength is renewed and I've found a new goal – to serve You. Your Word strengthens my faith; it has become the source of my hope. I will not chase my own desires and be led astray by the temptations of the enemy.

O Lord, do You hear my cry? It passes through Your house and sings:

"How great is the Lord? I can do all things in the Lord who strengthens me. Praise God, who found me when I was lost. Glory be to the Most High."

My zeal for You has begun to consume me. My soul trembles because of the power that resides in me. I will rejoice in the great name of the Lord forever and forever.

Author Reflection

As I wrote this chapter, "The Strong Tower," the Lord was changing the way I viewed my circumstances. Conventional wisdom tells us that success brings us satisfaction. This is not true! When Jesus comes into our heart and we align our lives with the will of God, we will find satisfaction in any season of our life. There is a purpose in every challenge we face in God, but it is our job to continue to obey His Word, be faithful, and remain still.

You Are Enough

The heart cries out from the wilderness...

Lord, in Your absence I will seek Your face. I trust You will never forsake me. I will silence every voice inside me and cover myself from the loudness of the world. Abba, Father, I know I will hear Your voice in the quiet place.

In this arid place I have seen the faithfulness of God. I desired to draw nearer to Him, and as I sought the Lord, He drew closer to me. At the moment I felt God's presence, there was a stillness inside me. I no longer cared for anything of this world; my only concern was the relationship I had with my Father in heaven. The Lord said:"For whosoever will save his life shall lose it: but whosoever will lose his life for my sake, the same shall save it" (Luke 9:24, King James Version).

Every burden I carried on my heart was attached to every carnal thing that I cared for. As I let go of my cares, my burdens followed. I knew if I wanted emotional breakthrough – so that I might strengthen my relationship with God – I would have to separate myself from my own desires.

I Am Renewed

Surrounded by the presence of God, the heart cries out...

Lord, You are enough, both today and tomorrow. You satisfy my soul and fill my spirit. I am renewed every day by Your power. By Your grace, O Lord, I was separated from the world and found my way. My desire belongs to You.

Your Grace

The heart cries out from the wilderness...

Lord, if it weren't for Your grace – the love that You've poured over me – today I wouldn't be free from this world's corruption. Your grace empowers me to overcome all things, to work efficiently, to walk according to Your will.

The work of God in a person's life is evident in their character. They are filled with His nature, called out from the world, and renewed in their heart and mind. Christ's sacrifice established a new foundation for all believers to settle themselves in God's promised agreement. As He was resurrected from the dead, He overcame the power of death for all those who come to God in the Son's name and turn from their old ways (before receiving Christ).

As we are brought into life, the Spirit of God makes us capable of doing His will by first changing us internally – breaking down the chains that bound us to our worldly desires. In essence, we are finally made capable of living our lives in obedience to the Word of God, not because we are under the law, but because it is established in our hearts and minds.

Greater Is Your Love

The heart cries out in love...

How wonderful are the gifts of the Spirit! They renew me and fill my soul; I am upheld by the countenance of the living God. It ministers to me on behalf of the Father (in heaven) and enables me to walk upright. Even now there is nothing of this world that has drawn closer to me. I have received God's love in its fullness, and in God's love is His power. His love restored me and filled my voids with the Word of life. Inside of me dwells the Son of the Most High; He is God's Word, and the life He brings has made me see the love of God.

Still Small Voice

Many times I am tempted, again and again. I am made weak. In the silence of the night, I hear a still small voice say to me:

"My love has overcome every power and authority."

As I distance myself from the desires of the world, I am drawn nearer to the stillness of my soul. The small voice becomes louder until it is the only thing I hear. It witnesses to my spirit and brings clarity. It fills me with a new desire. Every word it speaks brings peace, satisfaction, and healing. In its direction, I walk on solid ground.

My Cry at Night

The heart cries out at night...

My spirit rejoices, O Lord, in how magnificent You are. My eyes are set on You – my desire is to know You. I've seen You move mountains to fulfill Your promises. In the night, I heard You whisper to me. The firmaments proclaimed Your glory; the night sky sings praises to Your name. I looked up to the stars, and in the darkness of the night, You embraced me. You judged me according to my humbleness and gave me Your support. Abba, Father, You prepared a way for me; You corrected me and straightened my path.

What should I desire? What do I need? I have seen the movement of God in my life – His work is enough.

The Lord's Patience

The Son shines with much brightness and leaves behind no darkness in His path. He is merciful and slow to anger. I laid my burdens on Him and He revived my soul – His way is easy.

"For his anger lasts only a moment, but his favor lasts a lifetime! Weeping may last through the night, but joy comes with the morning" (Psalms 30:5, New Living Translation).

The Lord heard my cries and became my refuge. I will sing praises to His name, for He is the Almighty God.

Change

The heart screams out in the wilderness...

As I walked in my own strength, my weaknesses were revealed to me. I was thirsty, but where I searched there was no water. I circled in this arid place for a long time.

Perfection In Perseverance

In my time of suffering, the Lord began to witness to my spirit. He whispered, "I have allowed the enemy to tempt you."

"Why, Lord? Why have You allowed the deceiver to tempt me by my weaknesses so that I may be separated from You? Deliver me from the hands of my enemy and let me walk in the freedom of Your presence," I cried out from the desperation of my heart.

The Spirit of the Lord urged, "So that in your patience you may develop perseverance and be made in My own likeness. As you endure temptation you will be made perfect. But as yet, I am refining you by every trial you face."

In hearing this I came to realize that the battle I was facing truly was in not the harshness of the current season's conditions, but the hardness of my heart. The Lord brought me out of corruption and was now bringing me into His rest, but the journey was through the wilderness. James, the brother of Jesus, proclaimed:

"Count it all joy when you fall into various trials, knowing that the testing of your faith produces patience. But let patience have its perfect work, that you may be perfect and complete, lacking nothing" (James 1:2-4, NKJV).

To put it succinctly, it is necessary for every believer to face difficulties in order to mature. Essentially, the purpose of this season was to ripen my fruits (character) if I would plant myself in Christ by keeping His word.

Night Seasons

I will bless the Lord who has given me counsel; my heart also instructs me in the night seasons. I have set the Lord always before me; because He is at my right hand I shall not be moved.
Psalms 16:7, 8, NKJV

The Absence of God's Presence

The heart searches for the countenance of the Lord...

God, where are you? Even in the absence of Your presence, I know You haven't forsaken me. I am blinded from the blackness of the night. My hope is lost; I am in need of Your direction.

My Oppression

I have longed for water and found none. My soul has become like a wilderness. Where is the Lord who "secures justice for the poor and upholds the cause of the needy" (Psalms 140:12,

NIV)? The ground brings no harvest and the heavens bring no rain.

Spiritual Satisfaction

My spirit is without flaw. It brings me in remembrance of every promise from God. I am sure there will be no harvest in this season. Even the sky has dried up. But out of my spirit will flow streams of water.

"And you shall remember that the Lord your God led you all the way these forty years in the wilderness, to humble you and test you, to know what was in your heart, whether you would keep His commandments or not. So He humbled you, allowed you to hunger, and fed you with manna which you did not know nor did your fathers know, that He might make you know that man shall not live by bread alone; but man lives by every word that proceeds from the mouth of the Lord" (Deuteronomy 8:2-4, NKJV).

Part 2

Cries From A Place Of Redemption

SECTION 2

The Dry Place

The heart cries out from a place of redemption...

Lord, I have grown to understand the reasons why You brought me into this dry place. You are refining my character, first allowing my impurities to surface before You remove them. You tested me so that my perseverance would build patience. You tore down who I was and remade me whole. You revealed to me:

"The eye is the lamp of the body. So, if your eye is healthy, your whole body will be full of light, but if your eye is bad, your whole body will be full of darkness. If then the light in you is darkness, how great is the darkness!" (Matthew 6:22, 23, ESV).

The bitterness I kept inside me defiled my whole person. You changed my being and saved me from death. I am renewed.

Testing of Faith

Lord, in this season you've grown me in wisdom and understanding. I contended with my soul, endured in long-suffering, all for Your name's sake. I was conformed in Your likeness so that I would become a mature son of God.

Author Reflection

I've come to learn that in our spiritual journey, we will all be brought to a crossroad: We have to decide whether we want to walk in the direction that seems easiest, most desirable, and common, or follow the direction of the Spirit. The gift of salvation is received through faith alone, but our faith will be tested through our challenges in life. The Apostle Paul exhorts believers to endure through their hardships: "We must through many tribulations enter the kingdom of God" (Acts 14:22, NKJV).

In other words, Paul believes that it is necessary for us to suffer (emotionally, mentally, and physically) for Christ's sake because there is a promising reward that follows. In essence, we are brought through trials in our lives to mature us spiritually. But if we turn to what gives us gratification in the times that are meant for our growth, then we are only aborting the process.

Made to Know God

The heart cries out from a place of redemption...

"God, why have You abandoned me? Where is Your presence (peace)? Have I not obeyed You? You've left me to suffer in the aridity of the desert. I am faced with hardship; my soul cries out to me day and night; where is Your promise?" the heart cried out in agony.

Then the Spirit of the Lord said in an assertive manner, "I removed you from your place of despondency to bring you into Me, so that you may learn to trust in My character and walk not by sight, but by every word that I say. I made you in My own image; you were in My heart before I formed the world; My plans for you are perfect and My Word is unchangeable. My covenant declares: 'Every good gift and every perfect gift is from above, and comes down from Me, with whom there is no variation or shadow of turning. Of My own will I brought you forth by the word of truth, that you might be of a kind of firstfruits of My creatures' (see James 1:17). You were made to know me intimately, to grow in stature, and to mature in My character. So draw near to Me because I am your God! Anyone who delights in Me does not delight in the world. The spirit does not long after the things of the flesh, and the flesh does not long after the things of the spirit. My power (grace) has overcome every unnatural thing of this world. In the name of My Son, Jesus Christ, you have the victory. All who know Him also know Me. So do not give into temptation but endure through your tribulation knowing that My Word alone is sufficient."

Day and Night

The heart cries out in the midst of affliction...

Day and night my mind is unstable. O Lord, I am divided and broken. My soul is latched on to temporal things; I am made weak by my own desires. My soul contends with my spirit; I am never at ease.

"But You have seen, for You observe trouble and grief, to repay it by Your hand. The helpless commits himself to You" (Psalms 10:14, NKJV).

Day and night I long for You. My every thought is brought into submission before You. In my weakness, Your strength is revealed; Your power is transformational. God, You separated me from the world and gave me power over the deceiver in Your name. You made me worthy.

"For the weapons of our warfare are not carnal but mighty in God for pulling down strongholds, casting down arguments and every high thing that exalts itself against the knowledge of God, bringing every thought into captivity to the obedience of Christ" (2 Corinthians 10:4, 5, NKJV).

Day and night I found no peace. I've suffered for long; I am hated for Your sake; I do not belong amongst these people. I am rejected by many and accepted by few. They see my weaknesses and use them to subordinate me.

"You will be hated by all for my name's sake. But not a hair of your head will perish. By your endurance you will gain your lives" (Luke 21:17-19, ESV).

Day and night I suffered. I lived in my past tribulations. Before I knew You I had no place of refuge. I received the world and it brought my soul to corruption. But Your promise is unchanging and Your love searched the ends of the earth for me. You tested my faith in long-suffering but my flesh was brought into opposition with Your Word. The way of the world is gratifying but ends in destruction. So I will endure for Your name's sake.

"Blessed is the man who endures temptation; for when he has been approved, he will receive the crown of life which the Lord has promised to those who love Him.... But each one is tempted when he is drawn away by his own desires and enticed. Then, when desire has conceived, it gives birth to sin; and sin, when it is full-grown, brings forth death" (James 1:12, 14, 15, NKJV).

Day and night I seek Your face. Your way is life to my spirit and death to my flesh. It is painful and unbearable showing all my weakness and defects. I am brought into repentance because of Your revelation. You led me toward You even when I was against You. Your love brought division that separated me from every lie. I was unworthy, but You called me 'son' and I called you 'Abba.'

"Yet in all these things we are more than conquerors through Him who loved us. For I am persuaded that neither death nor life, nor angels nor principalities nor powers, nor things present nor things to come, nor height nor depth, nor any other created thing, shall be able to separate us from the love of God which is in Christ Jesus our Lord" (Romans 8:37-39, NKJV).

In My Weakness

The heart cries out in agony...

Lord, hear my cry and redeem me. I can no longer move forward in my own strength. I can't tolerate the pain; my life has no vibrancy, my strength has left me. I am alone, for those who hate You I am not amongst. All my days I find no peace of mind. My flesh tempts me to draw away from Your commandments, but I rebuke it. I hear the deceiver; he walks amidst the dead, calling me afar. Lord, give me strength and wisdom. Keep me from every lie, and tear down every wall the enemy has built up.

"Be sober, be vigilant; because your adversary the devil walks about like a roaring lion, seeking whom he may devour.... But may the God of all grace, who called us to His eternal glory by Christ Jesus, after you have suffered a while, perfect, establish, strengthen, and settle you" (1 Peter 5:8, 10, NKJV).

Abba, Father, minister to my soul. Let me be reminded of the days of my joyful youth. Yes, Lord, save me from the deceiver. The harshness of this season is too much for me to withstand on my own. I hide in the name of the Lord because You forsake none who come to You. Let the eyes of enemies see me prosper in Your name, so that they know You are Lord. You covered me and took me from my shame. So I will uplift Your name and say:

"Show me Your ways, O Lord; teach me Your paths. Lead me in Your truth and teach me, for You are the God of my salvation; on You I wait all the day" (Psalms 25:4, 5, NKJV).

Yes, the Lord redeems those who wait on Him, who live rightfully, and who love Him.

The Great City

The heart cries out from a place of redemption...

"Father, I will not give up on You. I was blinded by my own desires, but Your Spirit gave me clarity. You gave me a new heart and surrounded me in Your love. I surrendered to You and You showed me Your way. I found displeasure in what you find displeasing, in every mortal thing that brings corruption upon my soul like an infection over my body. All who have found life cannot find joy in dead works. I hate what You hate and cast away what You've rebuked.

God's Way

Lord, I am in great pain. My thoughts are captive to the desires of my soul. Father, do not let my path end in destruction. In my time of trouble, I will seek Your face. Without You, my walk is in vain and my labor produces no fruit. Your way brings forth life; anyone who doesn't know Your face is like a vagabond. The blind have seen good in their own way. They build cities by their hands; their hearts are filled with pride.

"Let them be caught in the plots which they have devised.... The wicked in his proud countenance does not seek God; God is in none of his thoughts. His ways are always prospering;... He has said in his heart, 'God has forgotten; He hides His face; He will never see'" (Psalms 10:2, 4, 5, 11, NKJV).

The Lord will judge them according to their works. He'll tear down their cities. But my boasting will be in the name of the Lord because He has prepared a way for me. I will sing praises to His name because He has heard my cry.

My Refuge

The heart rejoices in a place of redemption...

Give thanks to the Lord! He has brought me into His house and out of my troubles. My weight is lifted and I rest among subtle waters whose currents flow as the calmness of the day. When I was shadowed by the face of death You became my refuge. You saved me from the tempestuous winds of life. You set me on a solid foundation; my faith is established in You. You brought me satisfaction and fulfilled my walk.

"For when I kept silent, my bones wasted away through my groaning all day long. For day and night your hand was heavy upon me; my strength was dried up as by the heat of summer.... You are a hiding place for me; you preserve me from trouble; you surround me with shouts of deliverance. I will instruct you and teach you in the way you should go; I will counsel you with my eye upon you" (Psalms 32:3, 4, 7, 8, ESV).

The Cry of My Heart

I believed in the Lord and He secured me. The presence of God sheltered me. His kingdom is my foundation and I cannot be moved by the winds of affliction. I conquered all things in His name. My troubles withered away with the wind.

I desired You, Lord, and You took me from my place of shame. So I will rejoice in Your name. Amen.

Part 3

Cries From A Place Of Revival

SECTION 3

The Division

And it shall come to pass in the last days, says God, that I will pour out of My Spirit on all flesh; your sons and your daughters shall prophesy, your young men shall see visions, your old men shall dream dreams.
Acts 2:17, NKJV

A still, calm voice uttered to me...

I will outpour My spirit over the Church. Those who know My voice will follow Me when I call them. I will make a move on the earth, dividing the body, separating the righteous from the unrighteous, so that the secrets of men's hearts will be revealed by the words of their mouths.

The evidence that My love abides in a man is shown in their detestation of the world:

"If anyone loves the world, the love of the Father is not in him. For all that is in the world – the lust of the flesh, the lust of the eyes, and the pride of life – is not of the Father but is of the world" (1 John 2:15, 16, NKJV).

For many speak in My name, but I do not know them and they have no inheritance in My kingdom. But those who do My will and are led by the Spirit are My sons and daughters.

Dying to Self

I am calling all who are willing to die in order to receive life. All who come to the Son have found the Father. But all who keep their own ways remain in bondage:

"For if you live according to the flesh you will die; but if by the Spirit you put to death the deeds of the body, you will live. For as many as are led by the Spirit of God, these are sons of God" (Romans 8:13, 14, NKJV).

Again, all who receive the Son will receive the Father. For in Me there is nothing flawed or corrupt.

Author Reflection

Exactly three months from when I began writing this book, the Lord transitioned me into a new mindset. I was directed to begin a new section called "Cries from a Place of Revival," where the Lord began to outpour His Spirit into me; my writings were a reflection of not only my heart but also the heart of God. This chapter begins the section with a message that I was exhorted to write implicitly expressing how the Lord plants a seed in our life that we water through reading His Word, obeying His direction (see Hebrews 3:14, 15), and enduring through our hardships.

Forgiveness and Freedom

The heart cries out from a place of revival...

Lord, I will not be moved – I suffer day by day but I am not overcome. They see my shortcomings and are glad; I am resented because of the favor You give me. Their bitterness grows as I stand firm in Your way. They wear a double mask: their ways are cunning and their words are deception. Their hearts are never at rest; their love is in themselves alone.

But my forgiveness will reach their vanity. Was I indifferent, that I didn't need Your forgiveness? Hear my prayer, Father. As Your Son prayed for me, I will bless them and uplift them as Christ rose up in me.

Battle of the Mind

I can hear my soul cry out in distress. My internal contention is never at an end. A contradiction for every confirmation – a lie for every truth. But

I cast down every thought, depart from temptation, and lay down my own desires.

"Be transformed by the renewing of your mind, that you may prove what is that good and acceptable and perfect will of God" (Romans 12:2, NKJV).

I will crucify you, as He was crucified for me. Laying down my old life so now when I live, it is not me, but Him living in me. Putting every thought into agreement and accordance with His Spirit. My soul is torn down, victim to every tempest of the world, tempted by empty promises. But my spirit has no desire to accomplish anything outside the plans my God has for me. So I'll hold on to His Word and remain in His presence. I am faithful that I will see everything the Lord has promised me! I am patient in my suffering because I know the power of God is before me.

A Mighty Fortress

The heart cries out to the Lord...

Father, You have done what You've desired. Your Word hasn't returned to You empty. Your hands formed this mountain; Your Word has reached the depths of my soul. The kingdom of God has established itself in me. I stand in Your presence and dwell in Your temple. You've given light to my eye by the life of my soul.

"God of heaven will set up a kingdom that shall never be destroyed, nor shall the kingdom be left to another people. It shall break in pieces all these kingdoms and bring them to an end, and it shall stand forever" (Daniel 2:44, ESV).

The Division

As the Spirit witnessed to me I saw...

A mighty fortress (of the Lord) was set in the middle of a city. It was the light of the city, as the city itself was darkness. The darkness couldn't comprehend the light (see John 1:5). There was division. The light was Christ and the fortress was His bride (the sons and daughters of God).

The Kingdom

For the eyes of the Lord run to and fro throughout the whole earth, to show Himself strong on behalf of those whose heart is loyal to Him.
2 Chronicles 16:9, NKJV

The Fulfillment of God's Desire

The Lord spoke in my heart...

Humble yourself before Your God and lay to rest your burdens at My hands, holding your faith and walking in righteousness, that in due time I may exalt you. None who come before Me will lack anything good. My kingdom has come; My arms have embraced all who stood before Me. Their garments, torn from the battle, I have removed; and I have clothed them in fine linen. Blessed are those who reside in My house – pleasing in My eyes, for they're walking according to My commandments.

Blessed are those who have the right heart. Their way is upright; they are honest to their neighbors and loving to their enemies. They are the good fruit of the vine, a light in every dark place. Their love is the evidence of My power and grace, which bring life.

"For the seed shall be prosperous, the vine shall give its fruit, the ground shall give her increase, and the heavens shall give their dew" (Zechariah 8:12, NKJV).

Blessed are those who have laid down their life for My Son. He is the light, and all those who passed with Him now abide with Me and are given life as He is alive. So My Word hasn't returned to me empty:

"My sheep hear My voice, and I know them, and they follow Me. And I give them eternal life" (John 10:27, 28, NKJV).

I have made a place for them to abide in My presence and receive the fulfillment of My desire forever. My desire is in their hearts and their hearts are of My own.

The Light

The heart cries out from a place of revival...

As the sun went down, he rose to carry out his schemes. My eyes set upon the wide black yonder. Its skies imaged my soul's conflict with itself. I am blind to what is ahead of me. I hear his voice, yet again, but in the sound desperation.

"The thief cometh not, but for to steal, and to kill, and to destroy" (John 10:10, KJV).

I will not stumble and be brought into confusion. I do not serve myself; I submit myself to the Lord. He will be my light when the skies turn black. He will be my eyes when I cannot see. I am of one mind with Him.

"Then spake Jesus again unto them, saying, I am the light of the world: he that followeth me shall not walk in darkness, but shall have the light of life" (John 8:12, KJV).

In me is a place of abode for the Lord. He is the life that continues in me – I will not change my course. Though he may come at night, the light will guide me through the shadow of affliction.

The Covenant

I will give them one heart, and I will put a new spirit within you; and I will take the stony heart out of their flesh, and will give them an heart of flesh.
Ezekiel 11:19, KJV

A New Heart

The Lord's voice fell as fire and consumed my heart...

I sing praises to Your name with a new song in the stillness of Your presence. My soul is filled with peace and overcome with joy. The covenant of the Lord became my place of refuge; it was unfailing. So I will bless the name of the Lord and cry out, "Hosanna, in the highest," counting everything worthy in the name of the Son.

Who knows His promise? Who hears His voice? All whom He has called do not flow with the currents but against them. They will soar like eagles and will endure forever. Even those who have little will multiply what they have and it will become great in accordance with their faith.

All good things are in the covenant (promises) of the Lord. For those in His promise will be surrounded by His glory. No promise of the Lord is void – all God's promises will be fulfilled.

Part 4

CONCLUSION

Justified by Faith

But when the kindness and the love of God our Savior toward man appeared, not by works of righteousness which we have done, but according to His mercy He saved us, through the washing of regeneration and renewing of the Holy Spirit, whom He poured out on us abundantly through Jesus Christ our Savior, that having been justified by His grace we should become heirs according to the hope of eternal life.
Titus 3:4-7, NKJV

"Hear the Cries of My Heart" outlines a faith walk ordained by the Lord for all His children so that through the fire we may be refining ourselves in His stature and likeness. The process the Lord brings us through changes our "heart" and allows us to see our lives from the perspective in which God does. The Apostle Paul says in his letter to the Corinthian church: "We have the mind of Christ" (1 Corinthians 2:16, NKJV). Paul's proclamation sheds light on the matter of us being renewed through Jesus Christ and the Holy Spirit in our minds and hearts. To put this into perspective, we can come to the realization that as we are born again we will have a natural inclination to do God's will.

Paul refers to this as the planting of a seed and to the process as the water: "I planted, Apollos watered, but God gave the increase. So then neither he who plants is anything, nor he who waters, but God who gives the increase" (1 Corinthians 3:6, 7, NKJV). In alignment with the Lord's will, all these events took place. In addition, since we are justified by our faith and not by our works, the Lord is able to make an increase in our lives in accordance with our faith.

To complicate matters further, my walk in the Lord is then in obedience to his Word, which is done in the significance of my faith. If I were to live my life based on the knowledge of the world (putting it before the wisdom of God), then I would be working of my flesh (will), which can bring forth nothing of eternal value. Paul urges in his letter to the Romans: "For those who live according to the flesh set their minds on the things of the flesh, but those who live according to the Spirit, the things of the Spirit. For to be carnally minded is death, but to be spiritually minded is life and peace. Because the carnal mind is enmity against God; for it is not subject to the law of God, nor indeed can be. So then, those who are in the flesh cannot please God" (Romans 8:5-8, NKJV).

We can conclude that all those who trust in the Lord will be led by His Spirit, thus resulting in a way of living that is based from the standpoint of God's kingdom and everlasting life. Christians aren't perfect, but it is also undeniable that our lives are the makeup of the decisions we've made.

It is essential for us to grow in a walk of faith. The harsh seasons in our life prepare us for the promises that await us. No promise of the Lord will return to Him without being fulfilled. But then we have to ask, "Who will inherit these promises?" Jude writes: "But I want to remind you, though you once knew this, that the Lord, having saved the people out of the land of Egypt, afterward destroyed those who did not believe" (Jude 1:5, NKJV). Then, again, we see a reference in Scripture to the children of Israel's disobedience in the wilderness, when Paul writes his letter to the Hebrews: "For who, having heard, rebelled? Indeed, was it not all who came out of Egypt, led by Moses? Now with whom was He angry forty years? Was it not with those who sinned, whose corpses fell in the wilderness? And to whom did He swear that they would not enter His rest, but to those who did not obey? So we see that they could not enter in because of unbelief" (Hebrews 3:16-19, NKJV).

It is evident that in proportion to their disobedience was their lack of belief. A person's actions are tied in with their conviction and the condition of their heart, or inner self.

In conclusion, the refining process God brings us through is an uncomfortable journey that is known as a "wilderness season." Its significance is in building our character and spiritual maturity. I've learned that it can only be endured through faith. Job expresses his commitment to God as he says: "Though He slay me, yet will I trust Him" (Job 13:15, NKJV).

Because I am justified by faith, I am also empowered by God's grace, not by my own will, to overcome the power of sin. I am strengthened by the grace of God, not by my own strength, to be a conqueror of every stronghold and thought. I have outsmarted the enemy through the discernment of the Holy Spirit because I serve an omniscient God. It wasn't by my own knowledge. Paul writes: "But we have this treasure in earthen vessels, that the excellence of the power may be of God and not of us" (2 Corinthians 4:7, NKJV). The power of God will always be shown in the lives of those who trust in Him. Our trust is shown in our patience and obedience to the Word He gives us.

Devotional Guide

During my hardships at the beginning of my Christian walk, I wrote devotionals to the Lord. I came to learn to that in the harshest seasons of our life, we endure by deepening our roots in our faith in Christ Jesus.

In creating a devotional and consistently journaling my feelings and experiences, I was constantly reminded of God's promises and His unchangeable character. In the Old Testament, the prophet Habakkuk writes: "Then the Lord answered me and said: 'Write the vision and make it plain on tablets, that he may run who reads it. For the vision is yet for an appointed time; but at the end it will speak, and it will not lie. Though it tarries, wait for it; because it will surely come, it will not tarry' " (Habakkuk 2:2, 3, NKJV).

Habakkuk was inspired by the Lord to keep the visions (promises) He gave him written down and then further engraved in his heart and mind, so that even when trials came he would remember them. All God's promises will be fulfilled and are unchangeable.

In a like manner, I encourage you to do the same upon reading this book. I've outlined a 14-day devotional guide to help you write down your promises, lessons, and goals to keep a fresh and clear consciousness throughout your spiritual walk with Jesus Christ.

Let us begin!

Day 1
The Vision

Read: 1 John 3:2

"Beloved, now we are children of God; and it has not yet been revealed what we shall be, but we know that when He is revealed, we shall be like Him, for we shall see Him as He is" (NKJV).

Begin by spending time alone with God in prayer, and open your heart to see where He is directing you.

Day 2
The Promise

Read: Ezekiel 2:8

"But you, son of man, hear what I say to you. Do not be rebellious like that rebellious house; open your mouth and eat what I give you" (NKJV).

When the Lord makes a promise to you, the walk ahead will be a testing of your faith and obedience. Write down your promises. What will you do today to engage with God?

Day 3
What Have I Overlooked?

Read: John 15:5, 6

"I am the vine, you are the branches. He who abides in Me, and I in him, bears much fruit; for without Me you can do nothing. If anyone does not abide in Me, he is cast out as a branch and is withered; and they gather them and throw them into the fire, and they are burned" (NKJV).

God wants to manifest Himself in us, but we cannot expect to be productive if we can't see what is in front of us today. Start by writing down what the Lord has already done in your life.

Day 4
What Do I Appreciate?

Read: Luke 5:5, 6

" 'Master, we have toiled all night and caught nothing; nevertheless at Your word I will let down the net.' And when they had done this, they caught a great number of fish, and their net was breaking" (NKJV).

We need to always keep a fresh mind and strong hope in the Lord. When our eyes become fixed on our struggles, we can grow dry in trusting in the Lord. Remind yourself of what you're grateful for today and fix your eyes on those things.

Day 5
When God Moved in My Life

Read: Hebrews 11:6

"But without faith it is impossible to please Him, for he who comes to God must believe that He is, and that He is a rewarder of those who diligently seek Him" (NKJV).

Stir up your faith in the Lord by writing down a time when God moved in your life. Relive this moment and hold on to every promise God made you.

Day 6
What Am I Hoping for?

Read: Jeremiah 29:11

"For I know the thoughts that I think toward you, says the Lord, thoughts of peace and not of evil, to give you a future and a hope" (NKJV).

The Word tells us that God plans for us to have a good future. Write down what the Lord will be removing you from, and where He will be placing you. The change can be emotional, situational, psychological, spiritual, etc.

Day 7
What Does My Flesh Desire?

Read: 2 Chronicles 16:9

"For the eyes of the Lord run to and fro throughout the whole earth, to give strong support to those whose heart is blameless toward him" (ESV).

We are all tempted away from the will of God. But the Word says that we receive God's nature once we accept Jesus. Through Christ we have the power to overcome sin. Write down what your flesh is contending against your spirit to do and look toward the Lord to resist temptation.

Day 8
What Do I Need to Remove?

Read: Mark 1:4, 8

"John came baptizing in the wilderness and preaching a baptism of repentance… 'I indeed baptized you with water, but He will baptize you with the Holy Spirit' " (NKJV).

As we come to repentance and follow Christ, there is a process of sanctification that we must go through. Write down something you've held on to in your life that you need to remove in order to progress in your spiritual walk.

Day 9
Do I Have Spiritual Baggage?

Read: Hebrews 12:1, 2

"Let us lay aside every weight, and the sin which so easily ensnares us, and let us run with endurance the race that is set before us, looking unto Jesus, the author and finisher of our faith" (NKJV).

Evaluate yourself to see if you're being weighed down by distractions and write them down. These come in the form of thoughts, habits, relationships, addictions, and attachments.

Day 10
Where Am I Spiritually?

Read: Philippians 3:12, 13

"I press on, that I may lay hold of that for which Christ Jesus has also laid hold of me. Brethren, I do not count myself to have apprehended; but one thing I do, forgetting those things which are behind and reaching forward to those things which are ahead" (NKJV).

Where your focus is, is where your maturity is. Write down what you've been focusing on lately. Train your mind to continually bring yourself in remembrance of God's unchanging character.

Day 11
Distractions

Read: Daniel 6:7-10 (Scripture quoted below is verse 10)

"When Daniel knew the writing [making it illegal to petition any god or man besides the king for 30 days] was signed, he went home. And in his upper room... he knelt down on his knees three times that day, and prayed and gave thanks before his God" (NKJV).

Write down any areas of your life in which you feel you've compromised who you are in Christ. Meeting social standards is a distraction for many Christians. Are you one of them? If not, then reflect on a time when you demonstrated your faith.

Day 12
Temptation

Read: James 1:12

"Blessed is the man who endures temptation; for when he has been approved, he will receive the crown of life" (NKJV).

Remember that temptations come from the enemy. As you draw nearer to God the enemy will send temptation your way. First, write down the area(s) in which are you tempted. Second, write down the breakthrough God has promised to give you. Third, see sin how God sees it and identify how what you're being tempted to do will only become an obstacle in your journey.

Day 13
How Can I Show More Love?

Read: Matthew 22:37-39

" 'You shall love the Lord your God with all your heart, with all your soul, and with all your mind.' This is the first and great commandment. And the second is like it: 'You shall love your neighbor as yourself' " (NKJV).

When you are hurting, show love to others. When you need help, become someone's helper. Then trust that the Lord will do all the above for you. Write down one way in which you can show love to someone else and then commit yourself to doing it.

Day 14
Having a New Mind

Read: Ephesians 4:22-24

"Put off, concerning your former conduct, the old man which grows corrupt according to the deceitful lusts, and be renewed in the spirit of your mind, and ... put on the new man which was created according to God, in true righteousness and holiness" (NKJV).

We grow in our spiritual walk as we grow a more intimate relationship with God. Write down ways in which you can devote your time to God and then plan your schedule around them.

Scriptures

All NKJV *unless otherwise indicated*

Healing

James 5:14, 15

Is anyone among you sick? Let him call for the elders of the church, and let them pray over him, anointing him with oil in the name of the Lord. And the prayer of faith will save the one who is sick, and the Lord will raise him up. And if he has committed sins, he will be forgiven.

Mark 16:18 (ESV)

They will pick up serpents with their hands; and if they drink any deadly poison, it will not hurt them; they will lay their hands on the sick, and they will recover.

Acts 12:19

So that even handkerchiefs or aprons were brought from his body to the sick, and the diseases left them and the evil spirits went out of them.

Psalms 41:3 (ESV)

The Lord sustains him on his sickbed; in his illness you restore him to full health.

Self-control

Romans 8:2-4

For the law of the Spirit of life in Christ Jesus has made me free from the law of sin and death. For what the law could not do in that it was weak through the flesh, God did by sending His own Son in the likeness of sinful flesh, on account of sin: He condemned sin in the flesh, that the righteous requirement of the law might be fulfilled in us who do not walk according to the flesh but according to the Spirit.

James 1:12

Blessed is the man who endures temptation; for when he has been approved, he will receive the crown of life which the Lord has promised to those who love Him.

2 Timothy 2:21, 22

Therefore if anyone cleanses himself from the latter, he will be a vessel for honor, sanctified and useful for the Master, prepared for every good work. Flee also youthful lusts; but pursue righteousness, faith, love, peace with those who call on the Lord out of a pure heart.

Endurance

James 1:2-4
My brethren, count it all joy when you fall into various trials, knowing that the testing of your faith produces patience. But let patience have its perfect work, that you may be perfect and complete, lacking nothing.

Romans 5:3, 4
We also glory in tribulations, knowing that tribulation produces perseverance; and perseverance, character; and character, hope.

Acts 14:22
Strengthening the souls of the disciples, exhorting them to continue in the faith, and saying, "We must through many tribulations enter the kingdom of God."

Faith

Romans 10:17
So then faith comes by hearing, and hearing by the word of God.

Hebrews 11:6

But without faith it is impossible to please Him, for he who comes to God must believe that He is, and that He is a rewarder of those who diligently seek Him.

Love

Matthew 5:44
But I say to you, love your enemies, bless those who curse you, do good to those who hate you, and pray for those who spitefully use you and persecute you.

Luke 6:35
But love your enemies, do good, and lend, hoping for nothing in return; and your reward will be great, and you will be sons of the Most High. For He is kind to the unthankful and evil.

Obedience

Hebrews 5:8
Though He was a Son, yet He learned obedience by the things which He suffered.

James 2:24, 26
You see then that a man is justified by works, and not by faith only.... For as the body without

the spirit is dead, so faith without works is dead also.

Hebrews 11:8, 9
By faith Abraham obeyed when he was called to go out to the place which he would receive as an inheritance. And he went out, not knowing where he was going. By faith he dwelt in the land of promise as in a foreign country.

Promise

Numbers 23:19
God is not a man, that He should lie, nor a son of man, that He should repent. Has He said, and will He not do?

Isaiah 55:11
So shall My word be that goes forth from My mouth; it shall not return to Me void, but it shall accomplish what I please, and it shall prosper in the thing for which I sent it.

Hebrews 6:17, 18
Thus God, determining to show more abundantly to the heirs of promise the immutability of His counsel, confirmed it by an oath, that by two immutable things, in which it is impossible for God to lie, we might have strong consolation,

who have fled for refuge to lay hold of the hope set before us.

Discernment

1 Corinthians 2:11, 12

For what man knows the things of a man except the spirit of the man which is in him? Even so no one knows the things of God except the Spirit of God. Now we have received, not the spirit of the world, but the Spirit who is from God, that we might know the things that have been freely given to us by God.

1 Corinthians 2:15, 16

But he who is spiritual judges all things, yet he himself is rightly judged by no one. For "who has known the mind of the Lord that he may instruct Him?" But we have the mind of Christ.

Follow up with Taysean Wilson-Nolan's Work

HOURZERO

YOUR TIME IS NOW

WWW.HOURZERODESIGN.COM

YouTube Instagram

HEAR
THE CRIES OF MY
HEART

CPSIA information can be obtained
at www.ICGtesting.com
Printed in the USA
JSHW030013020920
7609JS00006B/84

9 781499 906189